Shawanda, Thank you! I appreciate your support — Felicia Baxley

The Help Meet

UNDERSTANDING YOUR CALLING AS A WIFE

Felicia Baxley

NEW HARBOR PRESS

RAPID CITY, SD

Baxley/New Harbor Press
1601 Mt. Rushmore Rd., Ste 3288
Rapid City, Sd 57701
www.NewHarborPress.com

Ordering Information:
Quantity sales. Special discounts are available on quantity purchases by corporations, associations, and others. For details, contact the "Special Sales Department" at the address above.

The Help Meet/ Felicia Baxley. -- 1st ed.
ISBN 978-1-63357-217-1

Scripture quotations marked "KJV" are taken from the Holy Bible, King James Version (Public Domain).

Contents

This book is dedicated to every woman who has the desire to be better. Every woman who acknowledges that she can always be better. Every woman who has the desire to be the woman and wife God has called her to be.

I especially dedicate this book to my amazing Great Grandmother, Ruth Elaine Baxley. I hope to live a long, prosperous life as you have, and to become at least a portion of the woman, wife, mother, grandmother, great grandmother, and woman of God you have been

First Revelation

"And the Lord answered me, and said, Write the vision, and make it plain upon tables, that he may run that readeth it." (Habakkuk 2:2)

Have you ever had a conversation with God that shook you to your core? A conversation so enlightening, so eye opening, you couldn't wait to tell someone? This particular book is encouraged by that type of conversation I had with God recently. I was driving down the road talking to God. I don't know if you are like me but I talk to God, especially when I am frustrated. So there I was, reminding God about all of the promises He had given me concerning this specific area in my life. I'm reminding Him of specific things He had personally told me about my current relationship, my future in this man's life, and so on. I was frustrated for the same reason I always am with God; the current situation seemed to look absolutely nothing like what He told me the end was going to look like. Here we are supposed to be married one day, yet today this guy seems to be showing no interest in me. We don't even have that "boyfriend/girlfriend" title anymore. And here God is, still telling me all of these positive things about our future. All things that seem impossible given my current state.

Has that ever happened to you? Has something crazy ever happened in your life and God doesn't address what you're spazzing about, He just keeps telling you about the good things to come? Maybe you've never been there. That's ok. Maybe it's just me who questions God. Maybe it's just me who can get pretty harsh with God sometimes. He did say we could present our requests about ALL things, didn't He? Then I'll even present His Word with my questions to try and make it less offensive. Is it really just me?

By this point, I've calmed down from the last time I had talked to God about this, but I still needed answers. I still didn't like the feeling I had. I didn't know what answers I was looking for. I didn't know what questions I should be asking. I simply asked God to say whatever He needed me to know. He did just that. I had to pull over on the side of the road because it was too much to type in the note section of my phone while driving (plus it's illegal to text and drive in most states you know). This revelation may not be as profound to you as it was to me, but you didn't pick up this book by happenstance.

This is exactly what God said to me. It's exactly the way I typed it up at that moment:

"God starts by telling me that He's trying to get more time with me now. Then proceeds to tell me that I can't be somebody's rock if I'm easily tossed or moved around. He said you keep going thru and going thru because you need to be unmovable. You can't be a rock that people can easily pick up and toss around. And you can't be easily blown away by the winds of life."

Then He says, "you have to learn to be his rock, and you'll have to prove yourself by your consistency. I'm like what do you mean? God says I created Adam a helpmeet. Out of his ribs. Ok God, why ribs? He said the rib is what protects the heart. It's sturdy like a rock to keep things from easily penetrating to the most vulnerable part of the body. He says I didn't put you with someone who needs a wife. I put you with someone who needs a help meet, and he's not going to know that for sure until he believes you can truly protect his heart. So while I called man to be the head of the house, the helpmeet (woman) is the one who protects his vulnerability. So the more you go thru and stick with the waits and tests, the more stable you become, the more unmovable you are, the more you're actually prepared to be the help meet."

In that moment, what God was saying to me made my Spirit leap. Don't get me wrong; I had studied what God's Word says about me as a woman. I had even studied what instructions the Word gives me as a wife. But it was that conversation with God that opened up my eyes to what the original purpose of woman was. Have you ever been WOW'D by God? Not that type of WOW you get because He did a thing for you. Not the type of WOW you get because He came through right in the nick of time. Not the type of WOW you get because He snatched the towel right as you through it in. I'm talking about the WOW moment you have when God reveals a little of His wisdom to you. He opens your eyes just enough for you to see something you have never seen before. That's the WOW moment I want you to experience with God, whether you have before or not.

Prayerfully this book allows God to do that for you. I believe at least one paragraph in this book sparks a new perspective for you. That conversation with God that day, driving down a rainy road somewhere in Georgia, shifted the way I saw my own relationship. It's my belief that by sharing what God imparted in me, it can help you decide how you want to view your own relationship.

CHAPTER 2

More Than A Title

"And the Lord God said, it is not good that man should be alone; I will make him an help meet." (Genesis 2:18)

Female was created because God saw a need the male species had. Let that sink in for a moment. God created the woman because the man was alone. God had man in mind when He created us women.

Over the course of time we have come to desire more as women. Some of us have come to decide that we don't need men to fulfill us. We have been hurt, neglected, and disrespected at the hands of men. I'm going to venture out and say we have strayed too far away from the purpose God created us. First and foremost, let's address the perspective we sometimes have when we look at topics such as this. God did not create us to be doormats. He did not create us just to cook and clean. He did not create us solely as sexual objects for men's pleasure. Nor did He create us just to reproduce offspring. Society and history have come to tell us what we are designed for as women, and somewhere along the way we began to believe this. Sure all of these things may be examples of the roles we may have as wives, as we will see later. This is simply, however, a distorted view of what God had in mind when we were created.

The idea of woman, from God's creative mind, is "an help meet." A helpmeet is essentially a companion or suitable helper. God created us with a characteristic and purpose in mind, not a title. God did not look at Adam and say, "You need a wife." On the contrary, He looked at Adam, noticed he was alone, and determined he needed a companion. He decided he needed someone to help him. God created a person who could contribute to the betterment of an already perfect creation.

Nobody goes around saying, "I'm his helpmeet." That defines characteristics. Instead we say, "I'm his wife." Even God called Eve a wife a few verses down. It's that title that we tend to seek, not fully understanding what it means for us as women. We don't understand the weight of the characteristics that should be associated with the title. We have spent time entertaining the sensationalizing of families for years. We all want the great American story. We want the husband, the kids, and the white picket fence. We want what marriage looks like from the outside when we view other couples. We want the freedom to enjoy and please a man sexually without the guilt and shame sin carries. We want a person who will always be there when we come home, the person who we can tell everything to. We want the assurance that we are and always will be the only one, the insurance that we so often assume marriage carries. We want love and compassion because that's what is supposed to come in the package of being a wife. We look at the TV families and we want a version of that tailored to our own selfish desires. We want what our neighbors around the corner have, the ones who are 105 years old and have been married 92 of those years and still seem to be happy with one another. We want the benefits that we believe and understand marriage to bring to us. More so, we want the title that affirms all these things, wife.

Being a wife, however, is more than being a title. The title doesn't guarantee us those benefits. The characteristics we hold however, can. We, as women, have made marriage a selfish matter designed to satisfy our own personal agendas. In this, we are missing that it wasn't a title God called out when He created Eve; it was a purpose.

Have you encountered people who desire the title of apostle, pastor, minister, elder, deacon, deaconess, evangelist, or prophet? They assume that the title grants them respect and honor yet when they open their mouths you can physically tell that their relationship with God is essentially non-existent. Their theology makes no sense, yet they flaunt the title around as if it affords them the right to say, do, or act in whatever way they see fit. I'm sure we've all encountered a person like this before. Titles seem to give people the basic assumption that there is an authority afforded to them that is not afforded to anyone else. People assume that when they obtain these given titles within clergy that it exempts them from certain tasks and qualifies them for others. Those simply title seeking are typically waiting for any and every opportunity to boast about the fact that they are what they are. I believe the term that may come to mind is "show-boating". The difference between title seekers and those called and anointed by God is that those without a title won't perform certain tasks without it, and will only fulfill the roles outlined within their specified description. Those anointed and called, however, are willing to do whatever is necessary to fulfill the will of God in their lives. Those anointed and called don't care whose job description it's in; they just know it's God's work that needs to be done. They don't need a title to justify what they do for the sake of Christ, and they aren't bothered if you never know they hold the title in the first place.

We can be like that as women sometimes can't we? We say we won't do certain things for the person we are currently in a relationship with unless they "put a ring on it." Ironically, we can often times be careless with the one and only thing God told us to set aside specifically for the husband, our bodies. We aren't willing to do the things that we feel demeans our feministic views or the things that make us too traditional, too close to barefoot and pregnant. We won't do these tasks. We won't treat that man in a submissive manner, yet we will do everything under the sun in the bedroom, or any other room we see fit at the moment. It's ok, the verbiage poses words like "we" because I'm not excluded from this thought process. I wasn't anyway. By no means am I saying that you have to fully submit to any and every man you enter into a relationship with. What I am saying, however, is that if becoming a wife is the goal you have, you shouldn't enter into a relationship with a person you don't believe you could begin to submit to.

It's not really about the man at this point. What I am trying to get you to see is that being the help meet will require more self sacrifice than you anticipated. YIKES! You mean to tell me I will be required to sacrifice more than I think I might have to? Yes. Being the character and purpose that God called the wife to be is so much more than the surface idea that society has placed in our heads about what wives should and should not do. I had to learn this the hard way. I'm not currently married, but I was. I am currently dating the man whom I know God has called to be my husband. You would assume that everything I have to deal with wouldn't be so harsh because I know this is whom God called me to be with. That's how we tend to think. That's what I thought in the beginning.

As women, we feel that the more information we have, the better equipped we are to handle the things that we have to endure. This is how I tend to feel anyway. If we just know who our husband is going to be or how long we have to wait for him, it wouldn't be so bad being single. If we knew the date and time God would deliver our current husband from that thing that is putting strain on the marriage we would be more willing to support him. If we could just understand why God has our relationships and marriages in the places they are at this moment we wouldn't complain so much or make so many wishes on so many stars for something different.

We can sometimes think this way even when we are married. The thrill of obtaining the title is withering away. The romanticism we once possessed starts to fade. Reality sets in. We've obtained the crown. The ring is on, and it's nice and shiny. All of our friends attended the wedding. Now our families can stop asking us about when we are going to settle down and find a man. But we didn't realize what the other side of "I do" looked like. We haven't been on the inside of those "perfect" marriages we aspire to be like one day. We hadn't prepared for the arguments because we didn't know we couldn't properly communicate with one another about deep cut subject matter. If God would show us though, it would all be ok. Let me take a moment to assure you that can be far from reality. Most of the time, yes it does help my faith walk to continue to trust in what God has told me the future holds. There are a lot of other "most of the times" as well. Those most of the times consist of me looking at the current state of my place in life, in this relationship, and every question I can think of is thrown at God because it looks nothing like what He showed me the outcome would consist of.

Title doesn't assist in these moments, purpose does. When a member of the congregation is struggling and they confide in the person with the title, it isn't the title that will determine if they can pray and witness to that person, it's the purpose and calling on their life. I understand that throughout the rest of the bible, the woman is referred to as the wife. What I'm more concerned about at this moment though, and the thing I want you to grab, is what was on God's mind when He created the woman. It makes for a feel good transition point in any sermon. It could probably even make for a great song. The fact that we were, and still are, on God's mind. It feels wonderful to know God is thinking about us. He is God. All-powerful, all knowing, all seeing, able to do exceedingly and abundantly, God. Yet He takes the time to think about you and me. But what is He thinking about? When He created Eve, the first woman, the first wife, the first mother, the first grandmother: He did so with a specific purpose in mind, to be a companion and helper. He thought about her in relation to how she could assist Adam.

Do you look at your current or future relationship that way? Is that the perspective you have on your marriage? I can assure you God gave me the revelation at the same time He told me this man would be my husband and I have still found myself repenting because I let it completely fly out of my mind (for longer than a few moments might I add.) The question you have to ask isn't just if a particular person is or was ordained by God to be your spouse, but what is it you have the ability to do for this other person? How can you help him? How can you contribute to him so that he is not only not alone, but also not lonely?

Let me share this with you. As I previously said, God already told me who my husband is. He also gave me the option up front to choose if I was ready for the work that would need to be put in. God, from the very beginning, not only showed me that I was destined to be the wife, but also all the things I was going to do for him. All the things I could do to HELP him. He also made a point to inform me up front (I'm talking not even a week into the "getting to know one another stage" up front) that this was not going to be an easy ride. As I look back on the many conversations I had with God thereafter, only once did He explain how this relationship would benefit me, and it still tied back to how I would be able to serve this man in the relationship.

That doesn't sound very appealing. Society still paints a picture of what marriage is supposed to look like. Fairy tale movies still give us the ideal of what the outcome is supposed to look like. Having the fairy tale perspective of love and relationships will set us up for failure and disappointing expectations every time. The truth of the matter is; we don't serve a fairy tale God, with fairy tale endings for our fairy tale lives. We serve a raw, uncut God who has plans to bless us in ways we would never have asked for, but still wants us to work on a few things. Being a wife isn't just about carrying a title so you can join the married club. It's also not about obtaining the status to live together or have sex without the fear of being caught doing something that shows you are still living in sin. It's about realizing the calling God has on your life, to spend the rest of your life serving another person and their needs. It's about deciding to be completely selfless to another person, and trust that God will be there for any area that you feel that person isn't equally contributing to for your benefit.

Eve was the first woman on Earth. The title meant nothing. Why? It proved nothing. There wasn't any other person their to need to justify the relationship to. There wasn't an audience that required her relationship with Adam to be specifically defined. We expect that title gives other people an idea of what type of relationship we have. We allow titles to determine boundaries and limitations on our relationships with other people. The title is simply to inform other people that a commitment has been made. It's an outward expression of what you should have already been living out. It's similar to baptism. We get saved before we get baptized. In today's time, there is typically a period of time that passes between when a person makes the confession of faith that they are trusting Jesus with their life and them being dipped into the water, symbolizing what has already been expressed. Don't assume here that I am down playing the covenant of marriage that God created between a man and a woman. I most certainly am not. However, I am showing you the root of the relationship of Adam and Eve and what caused God to create her in the first place.

The fact of the matter: Eve didn't need the title of wife, she was already showing Adam her commitment and loyalty to him by being what God called her to be in his life. This happened before she needed to be classified as the wife. God married them. There was no audience. Again, I want to make it clear that marriage does need to occur to reap the benefits God has set in place for this special covenant. Title seeking shouldn't be the reason we get married though. We should get married as an outward expression of a decision we made long before we walk down the aisle or go to the courthouse. The marriage should just confirm that we have already been serving and submitting. Symbolizing that we are a helpmeet. The title doesn't automatically give us the characteristics and behaviors of a wife. Those things should begin to be acquired well before a covenant is made.

If you have already made the covenant of marriage in your life, that's wonderful. If you are considering taking that step or hoping to one day, even better. Take a moment to reflect. Not on your current or potential marriage. Not on your current or future spouse. But on you. Reflect on the characteristics you currently possess. The current perspective you have concerning this area of your life. Is it what you believe it should be? If not, take a moment to talk to God. Ask God what you can be doing better. How can you be a better helpmeet? How can you begin to obtain the characteristics a helpmeet should possess? How can you begin to view yourself as the suitable helper of your husband or potential husband?

Prayer

God, I want to be whatever it is that you've called me to be. I want to live my life the way you saw it when I was formed in my mother's womb. Teach me. Show me. What is it that you want me to see? What is it that you want me to know about myself so I can do better? I want to be a helpmeet. I don't want to just brag about a ring being on my finger but I want to be what you ordained me to be in this man's life. I want to be the woman you set me apart to be just for him. Teach me how to be a companion. Teach me how to help. Teach me how to add value to his worth and not take any away. Show me myself God. Change my perspective and set me free from any area that is or has the potential to cause discord in my marriage. In Jesus name. Amen!

CHAPTER 3

Being A Rib

"And the rib, which the Lord God had taken from man, made he a woman, and brought her unto the man." (Genesis 2:22)

Men tend to show less emotion than women. Society has taught them for the longest men shouldn't cry, shouldn't show sign of any weakness. Men are strong. Men are warriors. They don't "wear their emotions on their sleeves" the same way we do as women. They don't open up the same way women do. Women were created from man, yet we don't carry the same characteristics as a man. We are only wired the same way they are in reference to physical structure, and there are even physical characteristics and functions that are different. So, why the rib? If you recall the conversation that I shared with you at the beginning of this book God had with me, this is the very question I asked. Why the rib?

If you took anatomy, or at least went over anatomy at some point in a science class like me, you may recall the ribs. They taught us that the ribs provide protection, support, and respiration. The rib cage is the structure that protects the heart and lungs. The heart and lungs are the very vulnerability of the body. The heart pumps blood to the rest of the body and the lungs ensure oxygen flows. Put another way, the rib cage protects the blood and breath of the body. All organs in the body are pertinent to the working of the vessel that we are, but these two organs were of such importance they required a sturdy surrounding. It was, and is, imperative to God that these two things have security around them.

This was so important that when God looked at Adam in the state he was in without a companion, it was from this structure that He created the woman. We already discussed that God had a specific purpose in mind when He created Eve; He wanted Adam to have a helpmeet. This still holds true when we look at the material Eve was created out of. Adam was created from the dust. Surely God could have created Eve from the same dust He created Adam, right? Of course, anything is possible for God. But had He created Eve from the same thing He created Adam they would have to function to serve the same purpose. Eve's purpose was different than Adam's, therefore, she had to be created out of something different.

Your mindset wasn't meant to match your husband's. You two don't have the same function in the Earth. You were placed together to carry out an overall assignment that God ordained for your relationship, but your functions in the relationship are different. This requires unique perspectives that have the ability to come together in agreement in order to get things accomplished.

Eve's purpose was further confirmed in what she was created from. She was created from a sturdy structure within Adam that is originally designed to protect two vital organs that kept him alive. These two organs are vulnerable if left open for attack. Eve was designed from the very structure that protected Adam's vulnerability. That's what Eve was created for. The helpmeet provides companionship and help to the one she is placed with. This help is rooted in the ability to protect specific areas of that person's life. Men find their vulnerabilities are very dear, and know that they are just that, vulnerabilities. These areas of their lives, if exposed, leave them open to attack. These areas of their lives have the potential to bring them to their knees, and even destroy primary functions in their life if left open and exposed for too long.

As a wife, we should already be helpmeets for our spouses. We should have already proven that we have the capability to ensure their vulnerable places are covered and shielded. The husband is described as being the head of the household. This doesn't mean that He holds all of the responsibility of the day to day inside of the family structure; it means that He is the spokesperson for the family before God. God deals with Him first in order to deal with the family. The husband is the provider, protector, and brings security. The same way we as women want the type of effort we give or better in a relationship, men require someone who can look out for them while they are looking out for everyone else.

It may seem like, or actually is that, you pray for your husband or future husband more than he prays for you. He is your physical protector. Adam had been hanging out with God and nature for a little while before Eve came on the scene. When she arrived, Adam knew that he needed to take care of her. This manifested more in the physical sense, because that's what Adam was created from, outer material. Eve was created from inner material. This gives us the innate ability to be more concerned with the internal of our spouses. We, as women, are naturally more concerned with their mental, emotional, and spiritual states. To us, it does no good for their bodies to be in perfect health but their mind or spirit is compromised causing them to fumble in protecting our children, and us. This causes us to pray and be alert in reference to what is contributing to our spouses mental, emotional, and spiritual wellbeing.

Man, this can be frustrating! If we aren't attentive, it can be a place that leaves us forgetting ourselves. We may be assuming that our spouse's prayer life concerning us is just as strong as our prayer lives concerning them. We seem to get attacked by the enemy more because our prayers are generally focused on our spouse or potential spouse. Let me let you in on a secret sister, we are supposed to be.

> *"And I will put enmity between thee and the woman,*
> *and between thy seed and her seed; it shall bruise thy*
> *head, and thou shalt bruise his heel." (Genesis 3:15)*

God stated there would be hostility between the woman and the serpent from the time of the fall. It was HER offspring and the serpent's that would be at war. Though the man contributes to the offspring, there was still a distinction from God that it would be the woman and the serpent essentially at war. Why? Because God created us with the ability to protect the very thing that the enemy would attack the most: our minds, our emotions, and our vulnerabilities. God created the woman from the concept of a structure already designed to do this. He purposed this for woman as He formed us to protect vulnerable places not easily seen from the outside. This purpose in mind, God spoke in the presence of the man, woman, and serpent, making it clear where the most hostility would lie.

So yes, you are probably attacked more times over than your spouse or your future spouse because that's how God ordained it. The enemy has to get through us in order to get to them. Adam and Eve weren't right beside each other when the serpent came. He waited until they were separated. Had they been together, Adam would have seen the serpent as it was, a threat. Adam named all the creatures. This means he knew their nature, and he knew their functions and potential. Adam's natural protective instinct would have kicked in to ensure the serpent did not harm Eve physically. From a physical standpoint, the serpent wouldn't have been able to approach Adam, because Adam knew the potential for harm. The serpent knew that the only way to make Adam vulnerable was through the one who protects his vulnerability.

If, by some force, a rib happens to break, it has the potential to pierce the very organs it is designed to protect. It requires extreme force to not only break a rib, but also break it so that it causes harm to the organs it is protecting or any surrounding organs. The enemy didn't physically attack Eve. Instead, he did what the enemy does; he messed with her own doubts, confusion and concerns. The only way for Satan to get to the head of the house, Adam, he had to go through Eve.

As women, we should already know that the enemy is going to come after us. It's not just because God stated at the beginning of time there would be hostility between us, but also because we are the protection. Our prayers bombard heaven on behalf of our husbands and children. We keep ourselves vigilant and ensure our discernment is at it's peak when it comes to our family. If we see any threat coming against our husband, or future spouse, in a way that we know he may not be able to handle like we can, we come against it. It only makes sense for the enemy to find the loose thread in us. If he goes straight for the weakness of the man, he risks us coming after him. We know how we are as mama bears, nobody messes with our family. Over our dead bodies, right? If, however, Satan finds the weakness in us, he can sneak his way not only into our minds, but into the lives of our spouses as well.

Satan manipulated Eve with her own doubts and concerns about what God had told her. This manipulation gave him the opportunity to infiltrate her, and moving on to Adam once the threat was addressed. Satan didn't directly go to Adam and have Adam eat the forbidden fruit. Instead, since he had already convinced Eve, he utilized her to get to Adam indirectly. What does this mean for us as women? What we go through isn't always about us. We have heard it before time and time again. We have been taught that our current trials and tribulations are for someone that we may come across sometime later in our lives who need to hear the testimony that we have. Looking at the role and purpose of the helpmeet, this concept goes a step further and is a bit more specific. As the helpmeet we are there to assist our husband's in whatever way we can, or in whatever way they may need within reason.

Understanding our role as the protector of our husband's vulnerability requires us to understand what may come against us. We are the barriers, in most instances, between our husbands and Satan. We are the walls of protection that ensures the man of God over our life is safe, even in his most vulnerable moments. This poses the question, are you prepared to take the brunt of the enemy's attacks?

Prayer

> *God, help me to understand the purpose you have for me as a helpmeet. Help me to understand what it means for me to protect my husband's vulnerable places. Help me to be willing to set aside my selfish desires and fleshly needs to effectively protect his heart. Strip me of anything that may cause me to focus more on myself, and step in when he is unable to reciprocate. Teach me to study your word more, and show me the design you had in mind for the marriage*

covenant. God, guide me in being aware of the purpose you have set for me in his life. Show me if I am falling short. Open my spiritual eyes to see the areas that need prayer in his life. Open my spiritual ears to hear his silent cries in order to war effectively on his behalf. God, give me a discerning spirit with wisdom to endure the attacks of the enemy whenever necessary. Amen!

CHAPTER 4

Being A Rock

"And the rain descended, and the floods came, and the winds blew, and beat upon that house, and it fell not: for it was founded upon a rock." (Matthew 7:25)

In so many movies and shows, we see the grandmother or mother portrayed as the "one who held the family together." Typically, if the female figure passes away, the family is in disarray. This may hold true even in some of our own families. We may be that thread that holds everything together. I have rarely, if ever, heard of the male family member being the one who was that thread (not saying that it is impossible though). We are naturally the foundation. We ensure the home is run smoothly. The children are washed, fed, and homework is done. Pets are groomed. The house is descent and in order. Whatever that looks like for each of us. Our husband's are submitted to and satisfied. We ensure the foundations of the relationships in our lives are concrete.

In the last chapter we discussed how important it is to be a rib. It was briefly discussed that we can endure the brunt of the enemy's attacks on behalf of our families. If we don't have a foundation within ourselves to understand what we agreed to, or are going to agree to, when we sign the marriage certificates, we are setting ourselves up for difficulties. The foundation we have is set within our personal relationships with God and our perspective.

> "He only is my rock and salvation; He is my defense; I shall not be greatly moved." (Psalm 62:2)

In order to be someone else's rock, we have to be sound and secure in who our own rock is. I completely believe that in a relationship, there should be a balance and an ability to be one another's rock. By this I mean that there is the capability for us to lean on one another for support. Rock, in this sense, is like a boulder surrounding us. Our personal foundation of rock must come first from God. If we go into, or are in a marriage, with the idea that our foundation is based on this other person, we have missed the mark. Man wasn't created with the intention of being a woman's "everything". Man was here first, and woman was created to complete HIM. We have allowed society and past hurts or pains determine that we don't need men,. We have decided they have to be all of these things if they want to be with us, but are we ready to be what God called us to be for them? This requires us first knowing that everything we need ultimately comes from God. He is the one who can and will fulfill our deepest desires and understand our darkest secrets, first. When we know God is our rock, our salvation, and our defense as the psalmist points out, it ensures we will be steadfast.

Being a rock requires stability. Knowing that the enemy is going to come against us, we have to possess the ability to stand firm in place. Rocks aren't easily moved. We aren't talking about the small rocks that you probably walk on in your driveway or pick up to skip in a pond. We are talking about rocks with the strength and stability required to stand. Boulders, mountains, volcanoes, caves, even Earth's crust is made of rock. These things aren't easily tossed about by natural disasters such as tsunamis, tornadoes, floods, hurricanes, or even earthquakes. We have to be stable in the same way in order to be helpmeets. We do this by first knowing God is the ultimate Rock. All of our help, inspiration, and example come directly from God, as He is the perfect foundation. He is always unmovable.

Being a rock also requires a unique perspective. This perspective will not be based in the depths of our flesh and emotions. We can't rely on what we feel, hear, or see in the physical realm to assist us in training and battles that are in the supernatural. The perspective we have to have has to be based in our relationship with God and our assurance for where we are in relation to His plan for our lives. This is first and foremost. Why? Because when God begins to show us things about our lives, our future, our spouses, we become excited and determined. It is much easier to endure the test and fiery trials of the enemy knowing that as long as we do whatever God has instructed us to do then we will come out on top. Having a supernatural perspective on our lives means that we can easily detect who or what we are actually dealing with at any given time.

For instance, when we are closer to breakthroughs than when we began there tends to be an attack of the enemy. Having the unique perspective of discernment allows us to realize that the fight we may be having with our spouse, the insecurities we may be feeling, or the trouble our kids are getting in to are just tricks of the enemy to get us distracted. The enemy doesn't want whatever God has planned to manifest in our lives. One of his most successful tricks is causing separation.

The enemy knows scripture the same way we do. He was hanging out with God way before all of us. He walks to and fro in Heaven, so I'm sure it is real easy for him to eavesdrop. This means, in order to cause maximum damage, he tries to ensure separation can take place. In separating, two or three are no longer gathered. In separating, the plans God had in mind for the two of you can't manifest with just one of you. As helpmeets we have to be aware. We have to acknowledge that the enemy wants to destroy things in our lives and he will do this by any means necessary. That small fight that other people may deem minute and not enemy related may be the very thing the enemy is using to cause disarray and separation. We have to be prepared to handle that. In the same way we typically look for the big and extravagant when we are expecting God to do something in our lives, we tend to only attribute large inconveniences to the enemy. We contribute deaths; lack of finances, and unstable employment on the enemy while these may just be the things common to man that life has dealt us. Or we have dealt ourselves. The enemy isn't really all that concerned with the big things all the time. Why? Because if he can catch us off guard in the small things, the small things will turn into big things on their own. He doesn't have to do that much work.

How does knowing this help us to be better wives? It gives us knowledge to address the issue in the manner it needs to be addressed. We can't address spiritual issues from a flesh perspective. Knowing when an argument, feeling, or thought is not just our flesh but driven by the prince of this world, we are equipped to deal with it in a different way. When we are focused on being the wife God has called us to be, we are more willing to call our emotions what they are and not allow them to determine major decisions we have to make. In Waiting or Warfare I discussed the body simply being a vessel and emotions being a necessary function of the vessel. Knowing that our bodies are the vessels, we are less likely to allow our flesh to control our relationships. This includes our emotions, our worldly expectations, and our own lustful desires.

To be a rock, we have to have this perspective in order to ensure we aren't easily tossed around and about by the winds of life. How can we be someone's rock if we are easily tossed across the world by a 2 mph wind? We can't. We would be too unstable to be considerate of the other person.

No matter how long you have been married or how long you've been looking to get married, God can always show you more of yourself. God's desire is that the union be ideal to accomplish whatever it is He wants your marriage to accomplish. Whether you are married or not at this point doesn't dictate when or how God uses your marriage. You could be like me. I know who my future husband is. We are in constant communication, constantly planning for the future, constantly pushing each other towards our goals. We have fun, we both have a relationship with God, we are both committed to allowing God's will be done in our lives. Those are all of the positive aspects that outweigh the negative ones. We both, however, also have work that needs to be done within ourselves to better our relationship. God is showing me, the future wife, what it means to be a helpmeet. Not a wife.

Don't shoot me for saying this but: Anybody can be a wife. If you can sign some documents and someone can bear witness, you can be a wife. You don't even have to be able to afford a wedding, just provide a signature and pay for the marriage license. It doesn't take much effort to become a wife. A helpmeet, however, requires more work. It requires more sacrifice. It requires more dying to self. It requires self control and discipline. At the root of a Godly wife is the helpmeet.

God's desire for us as wives is that we uphold our husbands. He designed us with the mindset that we would bring a special companionship to them that none of the animals could. It's amazing that God looked at Adam and said it wasn't good for man to be alone. God is omniscient, omnipresent, and omnipotent. Surely Adam wasn't alone, God was always right there. Yet God created woman to fill a void in man's life. God created woman with a purpose in mind; that purpose being how she would complete the man in a way that God wasn't going to. God created woman to help and build genuine relationship with man. That's what we are supposed to be doing with our husbands. Standing firm and being the rock our husbands' need is a role and characteristic of this. The question is, are we willing to put ourselves to the side for them?

Prayer

God, you are the Rock of my life. You have created me with a purpose and designed me with a destiny. Teach me now God how to be steadfast and unmovable. Teach me O God where I am easily swayed in my life. Show me where I may not be rock strong in my marriage, and then help me God. Help me to be strong. Show me how to be the solid foundation my husband needs. Teach me to be consistent and firm. Don't allow me to be easily swayed by the circumstances of life, disagreements, or others opinions of my marriage. Instead God teach me how to hear You in every situation. Show me what You would have me to do. Teach me to be submissive and assure me that I don't lose strength in being submissive. Show me how to understand what it means to be a rock to my husband and allow me to become that all the more. In Jesus name, Amen!

CHAPTER 5

Being A Gentle, Quiet Spirit

"But let it be the hidden man of the heart, in that which is not corruptible, even the ornament of a meek and quiet spirit, which is in the sight of God of great price." (1 Peter 3:4)

I don't often hold newborn babies. If I think back, there's only one that I have held before a certain time frame. Why? Because they are delicate. They require a soft touch. You have to hold them with the understanding that they are fragile. They are new to the world and very small. They don't yet have the strength or built immune system like the rest of us do. When I think of being gentle, I think of the care necessary to hold a newborn baby. Caring for something so tiny requires a subtle, gentle approach. You can't be as rough with a 3 day old as you would be with a 3 year old. Newborns are delicate.

If you were to ask any mother with a newborn, I'm sure she would tell you it's imperative not to wake a sleeping baby. It probably took her hours to get the baby to sleep, or she's trying to get their sleep pattern right. The result is that you can potentially hold the baby, you can gawk over the baby, but you must not wake it. This is where being quiet comes in to play. When we think of being quiet, we typically relate it to our kids or some other person making too much noise. There is something happening that is too loud for what we are prepared to listen to at the moment. We yell at our kids to be quiet. We tell the dog to hush. We turn off the TV. We do or say whatever we can in that moment so we can obtain as close to silence and peace as we can.

Being gentle basically means to be kind or tender, not harsh, and to be calm or pacify a situation. Being quiet is like it in the fact that in the verb tense it means to make silent, calm or still. In the way we typically use it, it basically means the absence of noise, or to carry something out secretly or discreet. Why does God hold these two characteristics as "of great price", and why are we talking about it in relationship to being a helpmeet?

As women, we tend to be jealous. We talk more than men do. We express more emotion than men do. Consequently we voice our concerns, fears, insecurities, and worries more than men do. Under the right, rather wrong, circumstances, this can be a bad thing. How? Let me give you an example. My future husband and I had a conversation very early on in our relationship about the fact that I do not, under any circumstances, like to be ignored. I can feel ignored in a number of ways. Since I am much better, or so I thought, at communicating than he is, I was sure to express all the potential ways I could feel ignored. This included what would set me off compared to what would just make me feel uneasy.

That being said, one day he must have been having a bad day. This was in the early stages of our relationship. We had a lot going on and I was still trying to figure out why God had me with this person to deal with what we were dealing with. I was having a good day. I called, within minutes he eroded with anger and hung up on me. Of course I called back. Ring ring, voicemail. Now if you could see the sideways look on my face as I type this, I'm sure you would know this means that the wrong thing had been done. After a few failed attempts at calling again, I got in my car and drove over to his house. Luckily, he wasn't home. [Don't give me that look either. I bet you have some stories too.] My anger however, didn't subside immediately, and since I am against causing bodily harm, I threw my phone. Hard. Screen shattered. Couple hours and about $300 later, we had a conversation about it. Come to find out, he misunderstood something I said because he was already in a bad mood. My response didn't make it better. Keep in mind; I was in a good mood when it all started.

That isn't one of the more "crazy" things I've done in this relationship. But I think we should get to know one another a little better before I go spilling all my crazy tendencies to you. I am sure, however, that you can relate. If not, kudos to you on harnessing your inner crazy woman. The point is: It's because of that inner crazy woman, that inner desire to be right and to not be the end of a laughing stock, that we have to train ourselves to be a gentle and quiet spirits.

Let's remember for a moment that the whole point of discussing what it means to be a helpmeet over just a wife is the role and responsibility we personally take in our husband's lives. We know that the helpmeet was designed with the purpose of keeping Adam from being lonely, with material designed to protect his vulnerability. Being a rib, a rock, a helpmeet means nothing if our husband's don't like our attitudes toward them.

It took a few years for me to get a revelation on this topic, one that would stick and allow me to effectively become a gentle and quiet spirit. It still takes a lot of discipline, but now that I am much better at it, I wonder why it took me so long to get it in the first place. As the helpmeet we have the power and resources to sway our situations and circumstances in a specific direction, or from a specific direction, at least as it pertains to our husbands. If you ask an older married man, or even talk to him for more than a minute and a half, I'm sure something along the lines of "a happy wife, a happy life" will be a part of the conversation. I used to assume that this always meant their wives had argued with them and made their point some time ago that the husband had just learned to let well enough alone and let her have her way. While this may be the case for some of those marriages, it's really not the husband's place to have to learn to leave well enough alone. Don't look at me too crazy here, a marriage requires work from both parties and communication and self-control is key on both ends.

However, as women, we have been tasked with holding certain characteristics: a gentle spirit, a submissive spirit, being made of the rib. These encouragements of our reason for creation sprinkled throughout the Bible tell us that we were formed more equipped to be self-controlled. We should be more likely to be able to diffuse situations. About 80% of the intense arguments we have in our relationships may be able to be avoided or handled more effectively if we as women are quiet until our own emotional state subsides.

The one thing my future husband has always shared with me is that he just wants me to be his peace. Let's not twist his words and assume he wants me to replace the peace that God gives him, however. What he means is simply, when things are chaotic and stressful around him, he doesn't want things to be so chaotic and stressful with me at the same time. Generally, men can handle all of the outside stress. For the most part any of us can handle a certain amount of stress at a time, it's when it piles on and comes from every angle that gets us. That's how it is for him. If he has already had a stressful day and I start coming at him with my emotions and insecurities that may contribute to him feeling inadequate to succeed at anything in that moment, things don't go so well. This happened to us a lot in the early stages of our relationship. We were going through a lot, I knew God had told me to stay and go through it, but since God didn't give me specific instruction I went through it angry, taking things out on him. How often do we do that as women? Or maybe it was just me, that's fine too. I learned, after spending a significant amount of time in prayer and letting

God reveal myself to me. I learned what being a gentle and quiet spirit actually was. I learned I was not that most of the time. So, I began to try to be a gentle, quiet spirit. But what does that look like?

For me, being a gentle and quiet spirit means taking emotional inventory and filtering what I say or ask. This doesn't mean I limit myself to what I can and can't say, it just means that I take into consideration how saying it would be beneficial to the current situation, and who it is beneficial to. Basically, I determine if what I say or ask, at this particular moment in time will result in an argument or misinterpretation given the current series of events. Based on that inventory, I make a decision on if it is something that should be brought up at a later time or if it something that I am likely overreacting to based on my own emotions or insecurities. This characteristic of a help-meet requires a lot of practice, self-control, discipline, and selflessness. It is simply a matter of deciding on the best timing to bring up a concern or issue and the best manner in which to do so. Sounds easy enough, but when you are in the heat of the moment, in mid offense, it can be difficult to do anything other than blurt out whatever raging sentence is erupting in our mind. This is especially hard for me because I don't do well with long-term confrontation. I don't believe in being upset or angry at one another for long periods of time. In my mind, we need to hash this out and come up with a solution, right now. That doesn't work for my future husband. He needs more time to rationalize and separate his emotions from reality before he can have an effective conversation. I had to learn it's best to allow him, and myself, time to rationalize those things before we sit down to discuss them. I have also learned that it doesn't have to wait weeks. It also shouldn't be left alone until another similar situation emerges because we were too afraid to go back to an uncomfortable conversation.

Being a gentle and quiet spirit is one of the major characteristics and skill sets God has provided us with specifically for disagreements and altercation. God has given you the ability to be the most sound minded and level headed in the midst of a disagreement, or on the opposite end of whatever may be causing your partner stress and discomfort. It sounds like a lot of self-sacrifice because it is. Marriage is a sacrifice, and it's up to each individual to determine how much sacrifice they are willing to make. To decide if it's worth it or not. God sacrifices everyday by remaining quiet when we lash out because He hasn't come through with that blessing yet, hasn't given us that breakthrough yet. When He watches us mess up and allows us to realize it on our own so as not to interfere with our free will. Sacrifice is required to be a helpmeet.

Prayer

God, help me to acknowledge that my emotions aren't always controlled. Forgive me for anything I may have gotten wrong with my husband, or anything I may get wrong in the future. Teach me, Lord, to be a willing vessel, not easily offended and ready to take whatever blow comes my way with grace. Hold my tongue until I can exhibit total self-control over my emotions and the things that I may say in the heat of the moment. Keep my spiritual eyes open to see the deepest need my husband may have at any given moment, despite what type of emotional states either of us may be in. Give me revelation into the Helpmeet you have called me to be, and allow your Holy Spirit to guide me along the way. In Jesus name, Amen

CHAPTER 6

Being Proverbs 31

"The heart of her husband doth safely trust in her, so that he shall have no need of spoil." (Proverbs 31:11)

We have all heard the term, seen the T-shirt, or bought the mug (and the bumper sticker). From all of the advertisement and recognition it gets, we understand that there is something about the character of the woman described in Proverbs 31. The woman in Proverbs 31 is the epitome of the helpmeet God had in mind when He created Eve. When He created Ruth. Naomi. Mary Mother of Jesus. You. Me. She is what we as women, devout Christian women, are (or should be) striving to become. But why?

Depending on the version of the bible you are using; there may be headings, subheading, or titles to explain to us as the readers what is going on. In the New International Version, right above Proverbs 31:10 it reads:

Epilogue: The Wife of Noble Character

Proverbs is known to be a book that carries much wisdom. At the end of all that wisdom, the most important thing that the authors', and God, wanted to portray was that of the character of a wife. A helpmeet. There are a number of places in the Bible where we find reputable women, housewives, warriors, mothers, and wives. There are also a few places where instructions are given to both the husband and the wife. But here in Proverbs, there are 21 verses dedicated solely to the character of this woman. It's essentially a written form of awe and adoration for what this woman accomplishes on a daily, weekly, and monthly basis. She has mastered all things helpmeet and here someone is ready to admire who she has become. The author has recognized that this helpmeet should be viewed as an example. She was getting things right.

Looking at it in today's understanding, the Proverbs 31 woman was essentially the superwoman of earlier centuries. Back when women were sure to be classified as the homemakers. The women who were essentially just "barefoot and pregnant." The Proverbs 31 woman can be viewed as that type of woman, to the naked eye. There is, however, a lot to be learned from this unnamed woman. Things even the most successful of us can be taught. You know, those of us who get up and go to work every morning. Those of us who are still in school full-time, while going to work full-time, while being PTA mom of the year at our kids' elementary school. You know, those of us who are the modern day version of superwoman. That's at least how others may sometimes see it. The woman portrayed in Proverbs 31 seemingly had it all together, like some of us try to, but in reality she was just content in her place of all the chaos.

In larger families, it's typically the grandmother who essentially "holds the family together." Grandma's have a way of cooking a twenty-five course meal, talking grandkids through homework she doesn't even understand, and reminding her own children about what task they need to complete. They do this without seeming phased by the chaos of it all. They've mastered it. They have become content in handling all the chaotic moments with peace and joy. Why? They know that as grandmothers, that's what they do. They help teach the grandkids things that the parents may forget to reiterate. They ensure everyone is sufficiently nourished. They know all of the ridiculous home remedies that are probably strongly discouraged by modern day medicine, but somehow work anyway. Those are some of the things grandmothers are known for, and they are content in doing all of these things. They have joy in doing these things because it's who they have become.

These women weren't born that way. They didn't come out of the womb knowing exactly how to cook a meal, help with homework, and clean the house, all at the same time without missing a beat. This wasn't the case. Over time, as they matured, they began to understand what helped the family function. Somewhere along the way they sacrificed so often it became second nature. Now, what once may have made them uncomfortable to do, they now accomplish with ease.

Proverbs 31, as we have discussed, gives us an inside look of the adoration someone had for this woman. It doesn't show us the sacrifices though. It doesn't tell us how much she sacrificed along the way to earn such adoration. It doesn't explain to us all of the frustrations that may have been associated with being adorned so much her story made it into the Book of Life. In the same manner, we may not be aware of the late nights grandma spent in prayer. We may not know what she learned to endure to be the woman grandpa needed, rather than person that would have appealed more to what everyone else wanted.

Becoming this woman, obtaining this type of character, takes time. It takes patience. It takes self-awareness. It takes sacrifice. We can't be like that woman without the help of God, not to it's fullest potential anyway. This woman in Proverbs 31 will teach us the characteristics necessary to contribute to us becoming the called helpmeet our husband needs. So what do these characteristics look like?

Proverbs 31:10 begins with the admiration of this woman with a question. A statement immediately follows that question.

> "A wife of noble character who can find? She is worth
> far more than rubies." (NIV)

It iterates the wife is of noble character and wants to know who can find her. The question, at first glance, is posed as if this is a rare occurrence. The statement that immediately follows the question is matter of fact. It further iterates the significance of her character by describing how valuable she is.

That alone should encourage you. Why? The purpose you have in your husband's life is valuable. That value is magnified when your character lines up with what God's placed inside of you.

I said that at first glance it would seem as if this woman is a rare occurrence. The fact of the matter is Proverbs 31 women surround us at different levels on a daily basis. You're already a Proverbs 31 woman. This holds true whether you have matured in every area of your life, marriage, and purpose or you are still growing. The rarity of it is this: My Proverbs 31 characteristics won't appeal to the husband God meant for you. My abilities are of no value to him. Why? God didn't formulate them with my personality and your husband in mind; God formulated them with my personality and my husband in mind. You are rare because you are the woman among all women that your husband had to, or has to, find. You become more valuable in your rarity, however, when you start maturing and developing in the calling on your life to be a helpmeet. Have you started developing into the helpmeet God called you to be? And again, what does it look like?

Trustworthy, with Good Intentions

Have you ever encountered someone who you knew you could trust with anything? What friend comes to mind when you think of a trustworthy person? What about this, have you ever encountered someone who presented themselves as trustworthy, but didn't have good intentions? Trustworthy can be the umbrella that a number of other characteristics fall under. If you were to take a few moments with me and check out

Proverbs 31 verses 11, 12, and 23, we will see in just a few ways this woman was trustworthy.

When an individual is trustworthy, you should be able to be fully confident in them. For instance, if I am fully trustworthy, you should be able to send me to the store to buy something with the full confidence that I will bring the item you sent me for AND your change back, right? This is what we see happening in verse 11. Her husband has "full confidence" in her. He can trust that when he tells her his most vulnerable secrets that she isn't going to go talk about it with her homegirls. He trusts that if he has a bad night in bed that she won't immediately start thinking about how someone else may be able to do it better. He isn't concerned with things that have the POTENTIAL to discourage her, because he has come to know her. He has come to love her. This means she has proven herself time and time again. He has started with small tasks and gradually worked his way up to the major leagues, and she has successfully come through in them all.

Taking trustworthiness to that next step, verse 12 talks about how she doesn't bring him harm. Her intentions are never malicious. She never tries to sugar coat something to look like it is good when she is just trying to get her way. She only does what will edify him, what will bring him good. There's that self-sacrifice again right? Because what may bring him good may not necessarily feel good to us in the moment. It's similar to when my future husband would always tell me he just wanted me to be his peace. He didn't want to have to deal with the everyday stress of life, only to come home and encounter my emotions had been going haywire all day and he is the only target I have to practice with. When we are easily offended, it can be hard not to retaliate. Thinking about his good, that can all go out of the window. But how trustworthy does that make us to them?

To our husbands who just want to sit in the company of their helpmeets in silence for a moment, can we be trusted with that task? Can we be trusted to pleasure them sexually, because at the moment that is for his good, even when we are too tired and don't feel like it? Can we be trusted to encourage them as our protector even when we are afraid? Verse 23 really hits home on the point of trustworthiness with good intentions. Can we be trusted to not bring embarrassment to our husbands, especially to those who are of higher standard that may be around him?

Being trustworthy is more than being able to go to the store, get the right item, and bring the change back in a timely fashion. It even goes a step further when we talk about having good intentions. It's more than doing that one thing for them only because we know we are going to want something ourselves in the coming days or months. Being trustworthy just doesn't include only the small or only the large things either. Being a trustworthy helpmeet with good intentions requires discipline. It's a lifestyle. It's something we do on a daily basis to ensure we are constantly contributing to the betterment of those we vowed to be suitable helpers to.

Not Lazy. Sacrificing Time and Putting Forth Effort

There are times I find myself seemingly exhausted. In reality, most of the time it's not that I'm genuinely exhausted; I would just rather lie on my couch and do nothing. Although I know I have things that should be done, that option is just always better for me. Maybe you're not like me, but sometimes I find myself being lazy. Sometimes I would rather not go out with my friends. Sometimes I may not even feel like going out with my guy.

I remember one weekend me and my future husband spent together. Ironically, every other weekend I want to do something or go somewhere when he is busy. This particular weekend, he set aside just to spend with me. He was prepared to take a little day trip out of town. Whatever I wanted to do. Do you know what we did that weekend? We stayed in the house all day Saturday watching football. I didn't feel like going anywhere. I didn't really want to get out and do anything. He was floored. The one time he was ready to hit the road; I just wanted to stay in. I was being lazy.

In Proverbs 31, there are about six verses that speak directly to this woman's sacrifice. They discuss her work ethic. Her ability to work and sacrifice her time to ensure she is being productive. Verses 13-15 talk about her being eager to work with her hands. They even discuss her waking up before the sun to get her day started. [I'll be honest with you right now, if I'm up before the sun, it's because it's probably the wintertime and it's now dark during my normal waking hours.] Verses 22 and 24 discuss her ability to create things, and verse 17 talks about how vigorously she works with her hands.

This woman isn't lazy. She sacrifices her time. She puts forth the work. She ensures that everyone is taken care of, no matter how early she has to wake up to ensure it's done. Sure, most of us are going to wake up and get to work on time because we have to. We are obligated to. But are we eager to do so? Are we working vigorously to ensure our family is taken care of? Do we take the time to ensure a proper meal has been prepared? Do we take the time to make the homemade version from time to time rather than the frozen version from a box?

Surely we understand that we should put forth the effort, sacrifice the time, and not be lazy during working hours. But let's take it a step farther. We are talking about this in relation to our home, specifically however, how does this relate to us helping our husbands?

You got up early. You made sure everyone was up and ready for school. You got the breakfast ready. You went to work. You came home. Made sure there was a hot meal on the table. You took the time to help your kids with their homework. You talked to your husband briefly about his day. You haven't been lazy, right? You sacrificed the time; you did the work, didn't you? But what happens when the kids go to sleep? Your husband's making obvious suggestions that he wants sex tonight, and you want to be the good wife to ensure his needs are met as well. But is it lazy? Do you put forth the effort?

It's often believed, and portrayed, that there are certain sexual favors we only do for our husbands on special occasions.

Birthdays, holidays. Whatever that special favor is, we know it's something he thoroughly enjoys. In those moments, whether it is out of obligation or as a present, we put forth the extra effort to ensure he is pleasured. Don't get too lost here. We are adults, and know that sexual gratification was created by God to take place within the covenant of marriage. So let's be real shall we? Do we spend most of the year putting in effort in every other area of our lives but are lazy when it comes to gratifying our husband's sexual desires? Sure, these particular verses don't apply directly to this particular subject, but isn't that an area we can become lazy in? We are too tired. It's been a long day. We aren't in the mood. Well in comparison, how often do you feel the woman in Proverbs 31 was tired, yet still woke up early in the morning to ensure a meal was available when the rest of the house woke?

No matter which area of our daily life, marriage, or household it pertains to, it's important that we take inventory on the efforts we put forth. Is there more that we could be doing by just sacrificing a few more minutes in the morning? Is there something productive that could be done that we are procrastinating because we don't feel like putting in the time or exerting the extra effort?

Financially Responsible

Oh boy! The topic society has taught us not to talk about much with others: our finances. We understand that God created the man to be the head of the household. Knowing this fact, we have fallen subject to societies standard of what the head of the household does. He's the breadwinner. He takes care of the finances. If he doesn't, or can't, he's not a man. But take a look at Proverbs 31 again. We just talked about her work ethic. Verses 16 and 18 take it a step further. She invests her money, which in turn profits her household.

She's responsible with her finances. She ensures the bills are taken care of. She works and earns money that comes into the home. She even takes the time to invest in properties that she finds are profitable. No matter what type of financial mistakes we have made in the past, because most of us are bound to have made some, what are we doing to edify our knowledge and understanding of our finances now? I imagine that the Proverbs 31 woman made a decision to be disciplined enough with her finances that she either helped her household get out of debt, or made decisions that would ensure they never got in debt.

It's said that one of the most common arguments in a marriage are over money. How many problems would be addressed in your marriage if the money problems weren't there? How many arguments would dissipate if where the next meal were coming from or how the bills were going to get paid were no longer a factor? We've said it time and time again haven't we? Being a helpmeet encourages the betterment of your husband. You aren't just purposed to encourage his ego and gently deal with his emotions. You are also wise. This wisdom can be applied to your home's financials in a way that can set your family up, rather than to continue to contribute to a lifestyle in struggle.

No matter what type of money troubles you may have now, you can help address and correct them. You can sit down and create a plan that encourages your husband to get out of debts. What about those of us who aren't in debts and don't particularly live paycheck to paycheck, are we still making wise financial decisions? Have you and your husband begun to understand investing to generate income and wealth? As we can learn from the woman in Proverbs 31, being the called helpmeet God has ordained even extends to the betterment of our finances.

Hospitable

Hospitality isn't my strongest area. This characteristic is one that may or may not directly impact your husband, but it is a characteristic that is of some importance. Verse 20 talks about this woman opening up her arms to the poor and extending her help to the needy. It can be difficult to sacrifice to and for people who may or may not directly affect us. Time and money are two things that are of great value in this world, and giving them to others can be a great sacrifice.

This woman did it. She was the type of woman who probably welcomed all the neighborhood kids in for a meal. She probably didn't mind sharing her work with neighboring women who she knew weren't as skilled as her. She may have even taken the time to sit down and encourage other wives how to be better helpmeets to their own husbands. All of these can be considered hospitality. I won't even insult my own existence by allowing you to think I am a very hospitable person. The truth of the matter is, I am not. This is definitely an area I am still working on.

Are you open with your home? Are you hospitable with giving money to those in need? What about taking the time to encourage a person, whether they are a friend or not, do you do that? How often do you heed the Holy Spirit when you're urged to sacrifice a little time or money to help someone else? This by no means encourages allowing others to misuse and abuse your ability to give. Rather, this is just another area that requires discernment and wisdom.

Fearlessly Prepared

Members of the military don't wait for an attack to start preparing. Military members from all branches go through rigorous training often in order to ensure that if and when the moment comes for war, they are prepared. The same holds true for sports players. The greatest players of all time, no matter what sporting event it is, train and prepare often. There is no such thing as an off-season; there is just the season where the game isn't being actively played. This is when the team has the opportunity to scout talent, learn from previous mistakes, and prepare for the team roundups they will face when the season begins again.

The woman in Proverbs 31 grasped that concept. She grasped the concept of being fearlessly prepared. Verses 21 and 25 give us insight into this. This woman was not afraid of the change in seasons, nor was she frightened by potential danger in the future. Why? She had spent time preparing. I mentioned earlier another book I'm writing, *Waiting or Warfare*. In that book I also discuss the importance of learning and preparing when everything is going well in your life for the inevitable attempts of attack from the enemy.

My future husband always talks about how he knows his purpose is to be a provider and protector. He fights battles for the sake of our family that I may never be fully aware of. What I do know is that he does so to ensure I am happy. The same type of concept holds true for me. I fight a number of battles, though they aren't always the same ones he fights. Mine are in the spirit realm. I am the one who is spiritually inclined and can sometimes see dangers that he isn't immediately aware of. You may be like that as well.

As helpmeets, we have already talked about the fact that the enemy may attack us first, in an attempt to get to our husbands. Spending time preparing for potential attacks is almost more important than fighting the attacks themselves. Eve was unprepared when the serpent came to her in the garden because she was unaware of how he operates. You aren't the same as Eve in this aspect. Surely you have encountered attacks of the enemy before now. Even if you haven't quite begun to understand how he operates, the Word of God is filled with examples of his character. God gave us His Word as instructions not just to tell of what He will do for us, but also to inform us of what the enemy's intent is. We already have the tools we need. We are designed to be fearless and to ensure that we are ready for any battle the enemy may bring our way. Sometimes, we may even have to take the battle to the enemy's front door.

Wise and Aware of Words

How often does your mouth get you in trouble? As women, we have the unique capability of killing hopes and dreams with the sharpness of our words. Surely it isn't just me. I can't be the only one who speaks fluent sarcasm and can cut through anything with words when I'm angry. This isn't what we should be doing with our words though. In verse 26, we see that the woman in Proverbs 31 speaks with wisdom and faithful instruction.

She allows wisdom to answer for her. She doesn't just blurt out the first thing that comes to her mind. Instead, she takes the times to carefully consider what it is her words have the power to do. This is another one I struggled with, but I am pleased to say that I have gotten so much better with it over the years. As proper helpmeets, we don't want to say things that discourage or tear down our husbands. That goes with being a gentle quiet spirit right? We don't want to insult or embarrass him by the things we say in the heat of the moment.

We have discussed what it means to have a discerning spirit and wisdom as a helpmeet. This is yet another area where it is necessary. Let me pause for the cause of pointing out that the only way we can obtain and properly use wisdom and a discerning spirit is with the help of God. Do you think that we will just be self-disciplined enough to ignore our emotional states and keep everything bottled up inside? Does that even sound healthy? Absolutely not! There are a few different things that have to be considered when we talk about being wise and aware of our words.

First things first, as I stated previously, we don't want to use the power of our words to intentionally hurt our husband's feelings. In the middle of an argument, we shouldn't point out this flaw or that flaw and completely discredit the work you've done to lift him up. Instead, it is imperative that we practice a healthy communication method with our husbands. It's probably not best for you to sit down and have a heart to heart when emotions are high. Granted if God blesses you with the innate ability to wisely have conversation in the middle of confrontation, you my friend, are blessed. If you happen to be like me though, allow yourself, and him, the opportunity to calm down.

Second, how do you handle feeling like you have the perfect idea that will help him do this better or see that in a different way? Let me introduce here a step in the communication process between you and your husband that you may or may not already adhere to. Prayer. If something is bothering you, as the helpmeet, the first thing you should do is take it to God. You can talk to Him about anything. He's your rock. Through prayer you begin to find out things. You gain more insight. Is it something God needs to deal with in Him? Is it something God tells you how to handle with Him? Or is it something God is trying to change your perspective on altogether? How many arguments could be avoided if we consulted God on the matter before bombarding our husbands?

Finally, this isn't all just about the negative potential in your words. As a helpmeet, there are so many things you can do to help uplift your husband; but are you using your words to encourage him? Being wise is one thing. We can all obtain wisdom. The thing about wisdom though, it isn't really relevant until you've put the knowledge to practice. You're wise enough to know that your husband is depressed right now, but are you aware enough that you know your words have the power to lighten his mood? Are you aware of the impact your words have at any given moment in time? This is all important to know for the potential of negative and positive language.

Watchful

This particular characteristic really goes hand in hand with being fearlessly prepared. Being watchful. Verse 27 talks about this woman being watchful over the affairs of her house. This means that if something is wrong, if something is missing, if something just isn't right; she is going to know about it. It can even go well with being financially responsible. Whatever pertains to her household, she is sure to watch out for anything that can go awry in it. It's the smallest area of our lives the enemy may choose to attack first. If he can cause $20 to be unaccounted for, he may have just caused enough confusion to enter into other areas of your life. As a helpmeet, it's also your responsibility to be aware of your household and watch for any potential areas of intrusion.

This means, you watch over your finances. You watch over how your children are doing. You keep watch over the company they, and your husband, keep. You even watch over yourself. Why do I say you watch over yourself? The second half of verse 27 talks about how this woman doesn't eat the bread of idleness. That means she is so focused on her own home, her own family's purpose, she doesn't have time to keep up with the Joneses. She isn't worried about what someone else's marriage looks like from the outside, because she already knows fully what she's working with in her own marriage. She doesn't try and keep up with how many times Mike took Jill on a date this week, because she knows what her own husband is able to do for her. She doesn't worry about how Sally was able to get three new cars this year, because she knows that she is managing her own finances and building wealth for her family.

I told you before; being a helpmeet is more about being self-aware than it is about being anything else. How quickly might the enemy sneak in and plant seeds of doubt and confusion if we are always checking out what the neighbors across the street have and compare it to ourselves? How many things in your house might the enemy be able to come in and steal because you're being watchful, but you're watching the wrong house? We have to be so aware of the purpose God has for our lives, for our marriage, for our families, that anything anyone else has going on is completely irrelevant to us.

Oh, Sue Ellen got a new car? Bless the Lord! What I'm waiting for must be on the way. That's the type of watchful we have to be. The kind of watchful that means we have heard from God, and in our anticipation of waiting for the thing He said He was doing, we can see the small things happening. We give Him praise for what He has done for our neighbor. We don't have time to worry about what is going on in someone else's life that's not going on in ours. We have to be prepared for what God has for us. So being watchful isn't always about making sure things aren't going wrong in your relationship, being watchful also means you are paying attention to what is going right. God may be blessing you right under your nose, but are you being watchful in a way that you can see exactly when God moves for you?

God Fearing

"Favour is deceitful, and beauty is vain: but a woman that feareth the Lord, she shall be praised." (Proverbs 31:30)

God is our rock. We can't do this helpmeet thing without Him. We can't do this life thing without Him. For me, this is my favorite quality of the woman in Proverbs 31. This is the quality that ensures all of the others work the way they are designed to. God fearing. A helpmeet has to choose to be obedient to God above everything else. A helpmeet is confident because of her relationship with God. Let me show you what I mean. As I put the finishing touches to this book, I still haven't gotten married, yet. But I am even more confident today than I was four years ago when we started dating that this is my husband. Why? My relationship with God confirms it. My conversations with God enlighten me on a daily basis about it. If you were to try and tell me otherwise, I would respectfully decline your opinion. I am so confident in what God has shown me that I cannot be swayed by any other opinion.

So how are you going to be able to tame your tongue when it comes to your husband? God. The more time you begin to spend with God, the more He is going to show you. The more He shows you, the more He is going to do things that just reiterate what He showed you in order to grow your faith. I found it interesting that it took the writer of Proverbs 31 until the second to the last verse in the chapter to mention her relationship with God. It's my belief that this writer wanted us to see all of the characteristics she was able to master. All the characteristics we may be looking at and wondering how will I ever get a handle on that? Then give us the answer. God. This woman wasn't superwoman. She was just super in tune with her God.

You can't just wake up one day and decide you are going to change every single one of these areas of your life and think it will succeed without God. Even if you are successful at it, it won't be the same type of success you will obtain when God is included. Because we live in a fallen world, things aren't as simple as they were in the Garden of Eden when Eve was first created for Adam. We have to put in a little more work. We have to give it a little more effort. We have to sacrifice a little more. Because this world is fallen and we are constantly in battle with our flesh nature, we have to have a relationship with God. One we are so confident in that we become immovable. All of the above characteristics will mean very little to your husband if you don't have the one that matters most, God.

All the characteristics of this woman directly affect the household. How do I know? Well, all of the accolades she was given were directly related to how her husband was taken care of. How her children were taken care of. Even how outsiders were sure to be taken care of if it was necessary. How would we do it? If we are always taking care of other people, who will take care of us? God. God took care of her. God walked with her. God created her for it, and she trusted Him to be her Rock. How do I know? She was God fearing! We already discussed it. She understood that if she let God take care of her wherever God saw fit to take care of her, it would be easier to submit to her husband, even if he wasn't affectionate enough at the time. She had gotten to a place where she was comfortable being who she was supposed to be for her husband, in the position she was supposed to be in her family, trusting God would take care of any area in her personal life that she felt was lacking. Are we willing to get to such a place?

Prayer

God, I want to be the woman you have called me to be. I want to grow and mature in the areas of my life that will increase my own value. I understand that I am so rare you have created me specifically for the man you had in mind when I was formed. Fill me now God with the ability to be trustworthy. Ensure I am not lazy God, but eager to do your work. Give me the wisdom I need to be responsible with my finances. Soften my hard to show hospitality, but give me the spirit of discernment and allow me to be watchful to ensure the enemy never takes my home. Most of all God give me a burning passion to begin to desire more of You. I understand that without you God, I may never be able to fully submit to the man You created me for. Allow me to give myself fully to you first, so that I have no problem with whatever it is You ask of me. God show me whatever area I need to be built in. Allow me to be self-aware and to acknowledge that I need You to help me in whatever area I am weak. In the name of Jesus, Amen.

CHAPTER 7

Can You Handle It?

"I have set the Lord always before me: because he is at
my right hand, I shall not be moved." (Psalms 16:8)

Being a helpmeet isn't always easy, at least not at first. Neither is being a parent. It's not even always easy to be a devout Christian. Being a helpmeet may not necessarily be easy, but neither is childbirth. We get through childbirth, however, because we have something to focus on. We have a purpose greater than the pain we experience during the birthing process. We wouldn't change our experience for anything, as long as we have the baby that we spent that time in pain to birth.

The fact of the matter is, we live in a fallen world. This means what our purpose and calling is in the eyes of God may feel contradictory to what we feel, or even what we don't feel, in our flesh bodies. Sacrifice is uncomfortable. Faith can be uncomfortable. Add the needs of another person to that discomfort.

Taking it a step further and ensuring you care about those other needs over your own feelings in the moment can be uncomfortable. Until it isn't. With most things, the more you do them, the more you become accustomed to them. The more you are accustomed, the more familiar the feelings and emotions you experience are. Once you become familiar with what it feels like to be the helpmeet, the discomfort is no longer paralyzing. It may even become easy.

No matter how long you've been living a life of faith; you're bound to have realized that the God way of doing a thing isn't always comfortable. Waiting on God isn't comfortable. Trusting God when the facts in front of you are contradictory is uncomfortable. This all holds true, until you get used to it. The more time you spend with God, the more He shows you His character. The character you can trust in. The more God comes through for you, the more comfortable you feel trusting He will come through again. The longer you walk with God, the more comfortable you become being uncomfortable.

It's rewarding. Walking with God is rewarding. Being a mother is rewarding. The same holds true for being a helpmeet. When you have kids, you begin to draw joy from your children's' excitements. No matter how long it took you to set up for the party, no matter how many kids attends, no matter how much it ended up costing you, when you see the excitement on your child's face: It's rewarding. When the day is over and all of the cleaning is done, your child gets to tell you how much fun he or she had. It's in that moment all of the frustrations that came throughout the day are now irrelevant. You succeeded. Your child had the time of their life. The joy of your child begins to bring you joy. It's rewarding.

The same should hold true for your husband. We mentioned earlier how we know most men don't like to be seen as vulnerable. Maybe he can't fully articulate how great something was that made him leap on the inside. Maybe his words and expression don't measure up compared to the level of effort you put in making that meal. But when you begin to observe their true body language, when you begin to take notice of the relaxation that has occurred and the subtle smirk of happiness that comes cross their face, it's rewarding. Or at least it should be.

There are so many of us who allow the frustrations of the day pile up and when the small thing occurs that iterates to you you are appreciated, you miss it. It's not packaged the way you want it to be. It doesn't always come in the form of a dozen roses and a teddy bear. It doesn't always come in a big hug and a "baby I appreciate what you did." If we were to become consistent and confident in what we were doing, however, we wouldn't be so easily frustrated to the extent that we miss the small cues that are silently giving us our accolades. We would be okay with the little bit of conversation he mustered to have with us at the end of a busy day, rather than becoming upset because we feel it wasn't enough. When we begin to become familiar with our purpose for him, and that God will make up for any difference we feel we aren't being benefited, we will begin to understand our husband's a little more. We will begin to know and acknowledge when the little we receive is all they had to give at the moment and they chose to give it all to us.

Do you want to hear something crazy about being a help-meet? I mean, in addition to the things I've already said that probably seem a little crazy right now. Being a helpmeet doesn't start with you having a husband. It doesn't start with the signing of the marriage license. It doesn't start with the "I do". It doesn't even start when you begin dating the fella who is to be your husband. Not even when you become engaged. Being a helpmeet starts with you. It begins with your decision that you are willing to self-sacrifice to whatever extent God deems necessary for the betterment of your husband.

Whether you've been married for years or you haven't even held a consistent long-term relationship, you won't ever be able to reach your fullest potential as the suitable helper for your husband until the decision is made. Until you determine in your heart of hearts that you are willing to do everything is takes to be the woman God has called you to be, for the betterment of the man He had in mind when He created you: You'll always be valuable, but not rare. It can sound a little crazy at first. If I were to be completely transparent with you, I've had this great revelation from God, and I still struggle with it from time to time. You have to willingly make the decision to be uncomfortable, to whatever extent God allows, for the betterment of someone else. Not just anyone else, a man. The man. The man God thought about when He formed you. And it's not for "his sake", it's for his betterment. It's for his growth and development. It's to make what God already created to be valuable even more valuable. It's to make him complete.

The real question I pose to you at this moment in time is: Can you handle it? Are you ready to make that sacrifice? Are you ready to make the decision to put yourself in a position that may make you uncomfortable? If you don't think so at the moment that's okay. If you're already married, and have been for years, and find yourself in a position that you aren't even sure if you are ready for this kind of purpose, that's okay. I do believe, however, that you wouldn't have picked up this book, and read all the way to this section if you didn't have at least the desire.

There are a lot of things we talked about during our short, or long, time together. Telling God that you are ready and willing does not mean that each and every area of your life will need to change dramatically in a short amount of time. The great thing about the God we serve is that He will work with even the faintest of our desires to ensure His will comes to pass. The entire first step is being upfront and honest with God, and yourself, about where you may have fallen short. Telling God what has stood out to you in this book and what areas you know you need to work on. Expressing the desire to Him that you want to live in the purpose He called you to. You want to better your husband, but you don't know how. That's the first step in enhancing your marriage. That's the first step in what can become total restoration if need be.

I don't have a prayer for this last chapter. This is where it's your turn. It's your turn to speak directly to God. Be open and honest with Him about your desire to be a helpmeet. Open up to Him about where you think you fall short. Talk to Him about what you feel a marriage should look like. Then listen. What is it your Father wants you to know about how suitable you are?

About The Author

Growing up in a small town in Georgia, Felicia began writing when she was in elementary school. Even before she found God she was able to put words to paper in an effort to relieve her own anxieties and depression. As she grew older, she began to write more and more as an outlet to relieve that anxiety and depression. Well after she had begun to manage her anger, well after she had learned to manage her anxiety, well after she had stopped writing altogether, God reminded her of that ability to write. It was then that God revealed his purpose for her to continue writing. Felicia is now fully confident in her calling to put words to paper in an effort to spread the revelations, knowledge, and wisdom God shares with her. Though this is only her first published work, there are a number of writings to come that she is fully confident are God-breathed.

For more information about the author, business inquiries, or donations please contact Felicia at feliciabtheauthor@gmail.com

Upcoming Titles

Waiting or Warfare

God Crazy

After Deliverance, Before Destiny

CPSIA information can be obtained
at www.ICGtesting.com
Printed in the USA
BVHW031452260120
570505BV00001B/63

9 781633 572171